slippers

juice

ball

plane

strawberries

park

first 200 words

bike

hamburger

crayons

bath tub

boy

sneakers

© Evans Brilliant

All rights are reserved. No part of this publication may be reproduced, stored in a retrieval system or transmitted in any form or by any means, electronic, mechanical, photocopying, recording or otherwise, without prior permission

 biscuit	 bread	 butter
 cake	**Food** 	 cereal
 cheese	 chips	 egg

hamburger

ice cream

meat

milk

Food

pizza

soup

spaghetti

cupcake

 water	 juice	 soda
 milkshake	 **Drink**	 coffee
 tea	 hot chocolate	 Strawberry milk

 apple	 banana	 grapes
 orange	 # Fruits	 pear
 strawberries	 cherries	 mango

 carrot	 potatoes	 corn
 peas	 **Vegetables**	 lettuce
 mushroom	 spinach	 cucumber

 pumpkin	 broccoli	 zucchini (us) courgette (uk)
 eggplant	 **Vegetables**	 tomato
 beans	 onion	 raddish

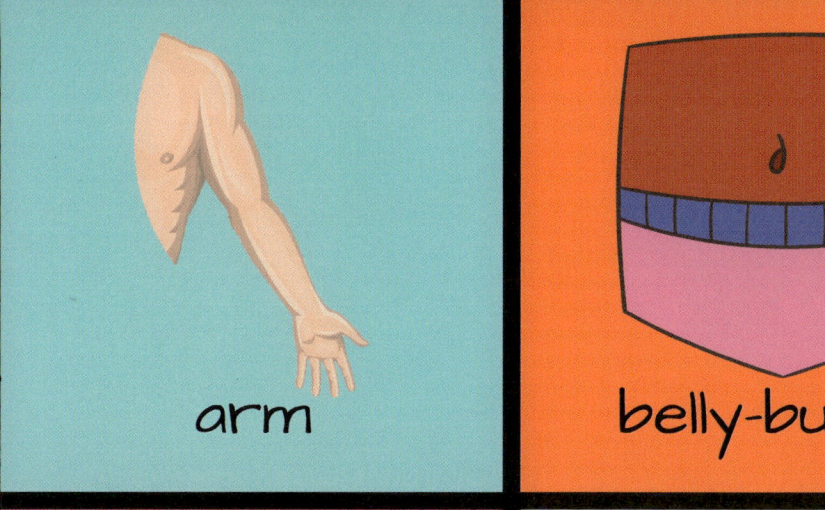 arm	 belly-button	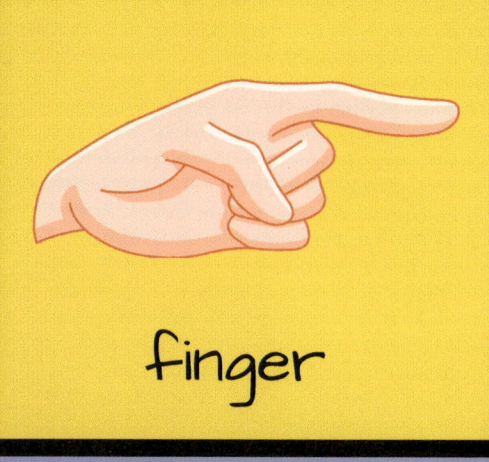 finger
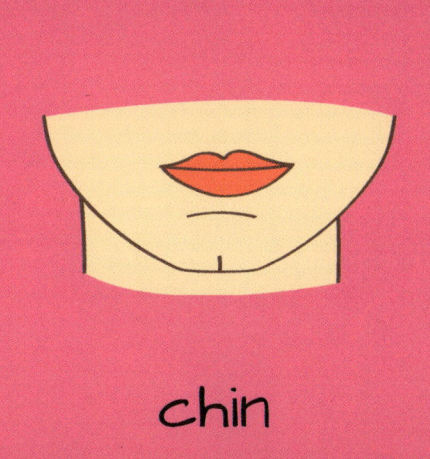 chin	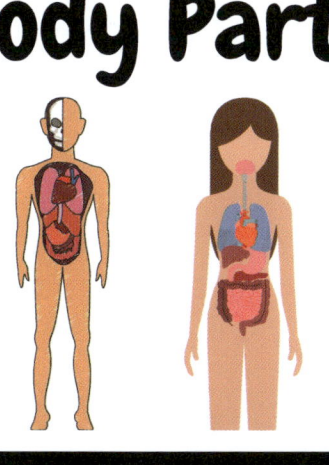 **Body Parts**	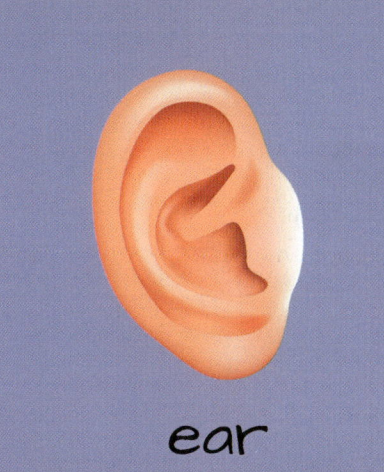 ear
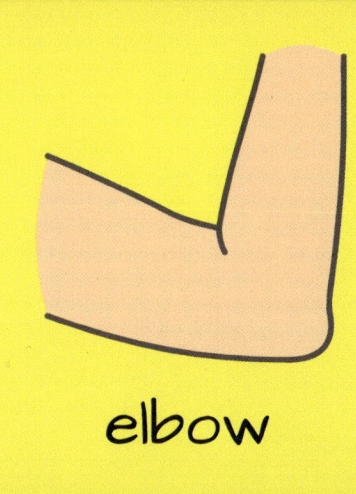 elbow	 eye	 face

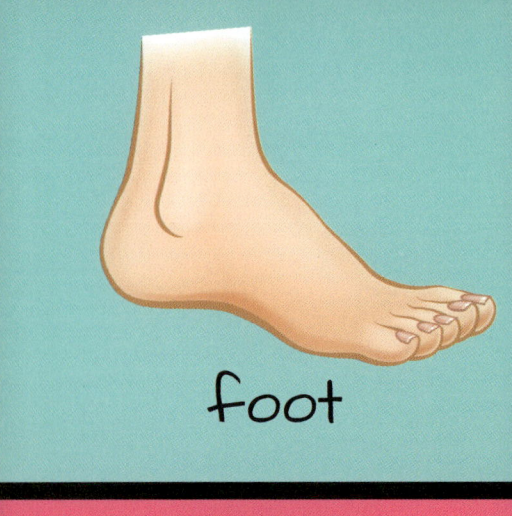
foot

hair

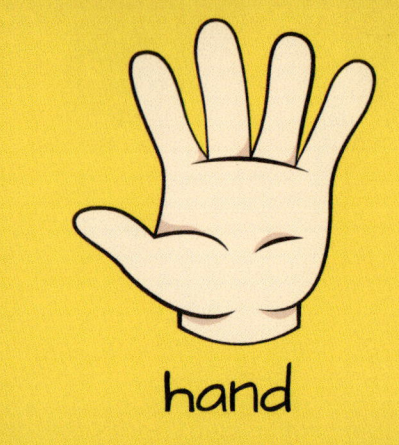
hand

head

Body Parts

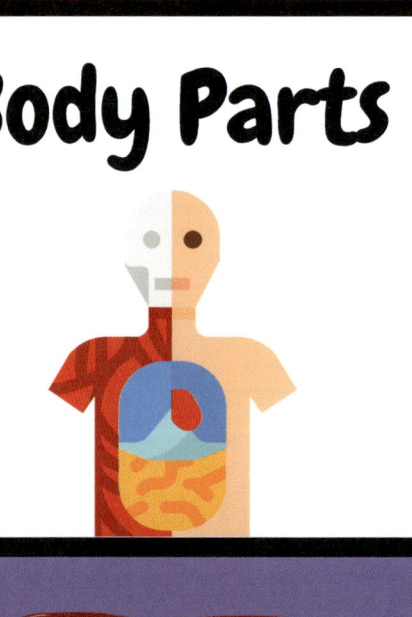

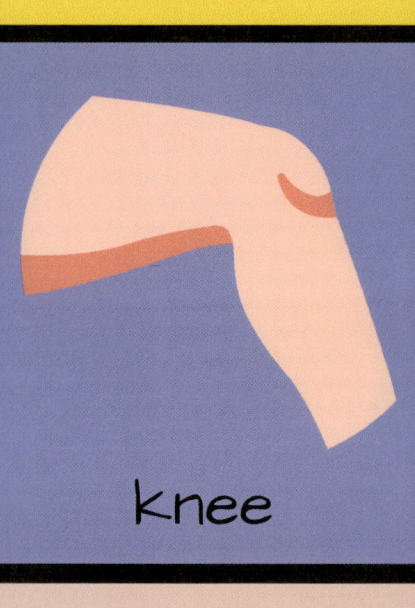
knee

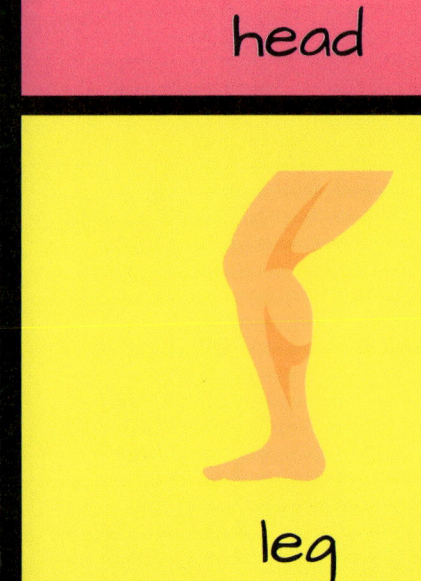
leg

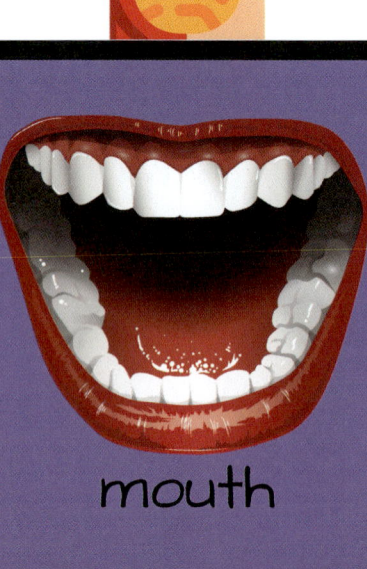
mouth

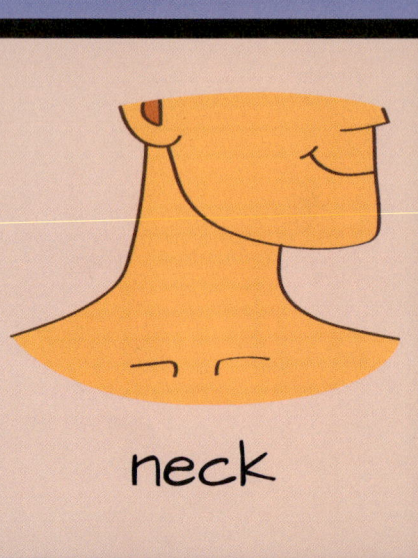
neck

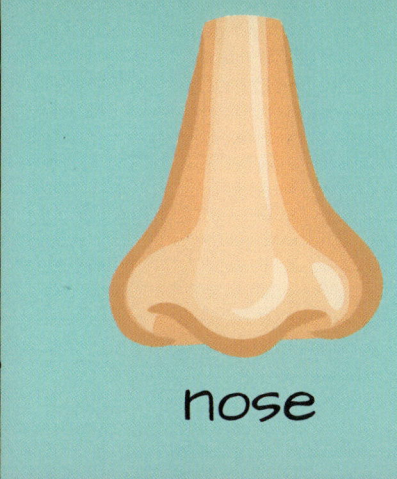 nose	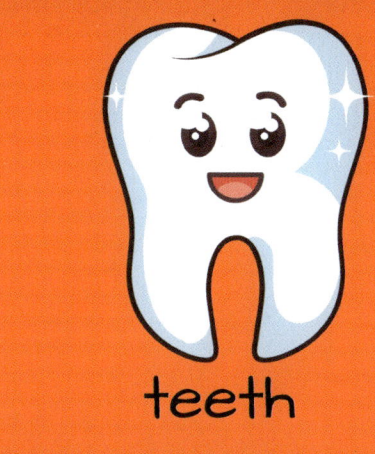 teeth	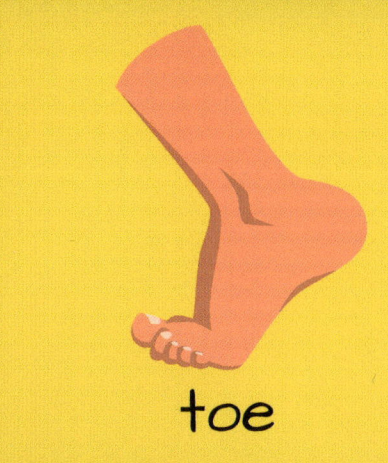 toe
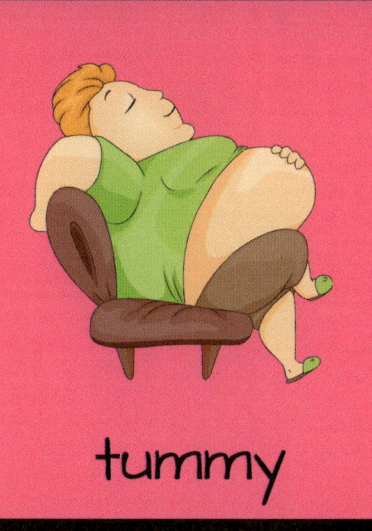 tummy	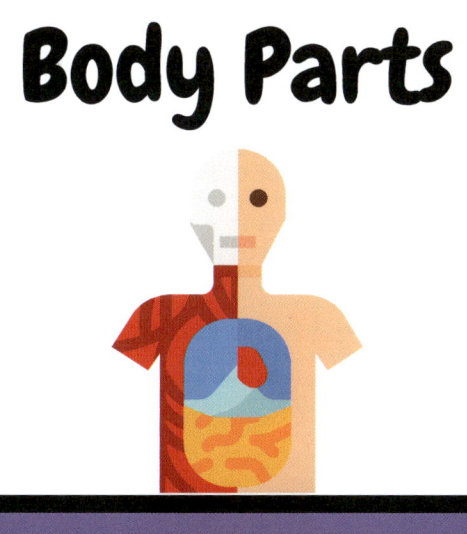 Body Parts	 torso
 buttock	 beard	 mustache

blue	green	yellow
red	**Colors**	orange
brown	purple	gray

pink	black	white
golden	**Colors**	silver
peach	turquoise	berry

 home	 hospital	 library
 park	# Places 	 school
 shop	 zoo	 swimming pool

 ball	 blocks	 book
 bubble	 Toys	 crayons
 doll	 gift (us) present (uk)	 teddy bear

 bike	 bus	 boat
 car	 Vehicles	 plane
 tractor	 train	 truck

flower

footpath

house

moon

Outdoors

rain

snow

star

street

 aunt	 baby	 boy
 daddy	 People	 doctor
 girl	 grandma	 grandpa

 lady	 man	 mommy (us) mummy (uk)
 sister	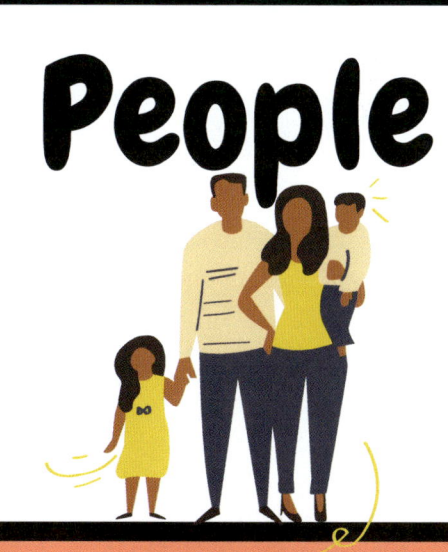 People	 uncle
 teacher	 friends	 brother

 bed	 blanket	 bottle
 bowl	## Household 	 chair
 clock	 cot	 cup

 door	 floor	 fork
 glass	**Household** 	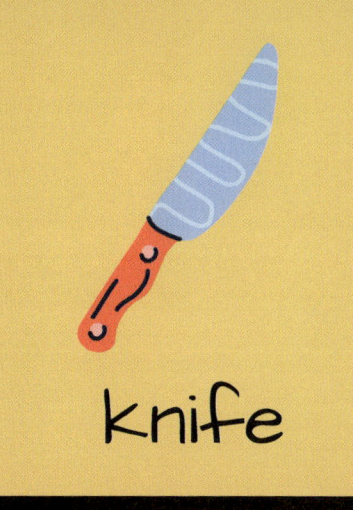 knife
 light	 mirror	 pillow

 plate	 radio	 rubbish
 sink	 Household	 soap
 spoon	 stairs	 table

 kitchen	 bathroom	 bedroom
 living room	 **At home**	 dining room
 nursery	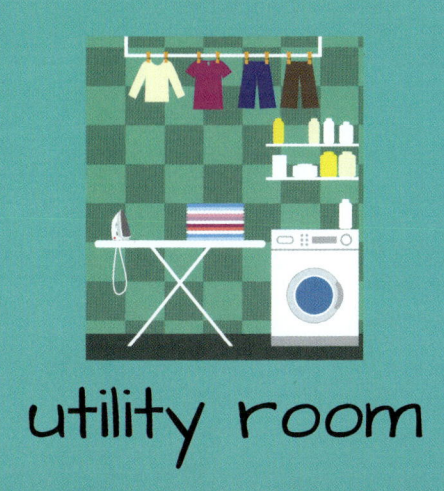 utility room	 garage

 **bath tub**	 **brush**	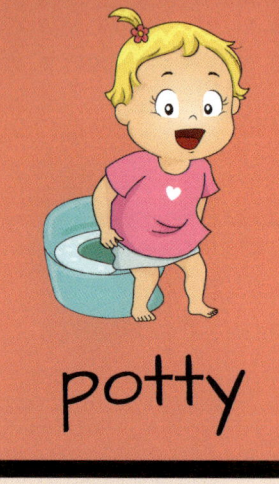 **potty**
 **toilet paper**	# Bathtime 	 **wash**
 **boat**	 **towel**	 **duck**

love

run

eat

dance

Action

sleep

sing

sit

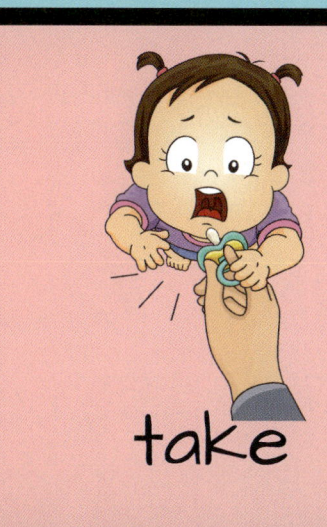
take

boots

coat

gloves

hat

Clothes

jumper

nappy

pyjamas

dress

 pants	 shirt	 shoes
 slippers	 **Clothes**	 sneakers
 socks	 t-hirt	 short pants

Printed in Great Britain
by Amazon